Abraham, Sarah, & Isaac

The story of Abraham's faith in God for children

Based on Genesis 15:1–6; 17:15–19; 21:1–7; and 22:1–18

Written by Joanne Bader

Illustrated by Ed Koehler

CONCORDIA PUBLISHING HOUSE · SAINT LOUIS

Long ago in a distant land
There lived a righteous man.
He had great faith in God the Lord.
He knew God had a plan.

This man whose name was Abraham
Was blessed with many things,
Like servants, cattle, sheep, and goats,
And gold and silver rings.

He had a faithful, loving wife,
And Sarah was her name.
She had no children of her own.
It made her feel great shame.

God promised this to Abraham,
"Someday your family
Will number more than stars above
Or sand that's near the sea."

How can that be, thought Abraham,
We have no children now.
*I'm sure we are too **old** for kids,*
But I believe God's vow.

Then one day God appeared to him
To Abraham He said,
"Quite soon your wife will bear a son.
He'll follow in your stead."

Within a year Isaac was born
Just as God said he'd be.
So Abraham and Sarah, too,
Were filled with joy and glee.

They knew that they'd been richly blessed.
Their thankful hearts were glad.
They watched their dear son, Isaac, grow
Into a fine young lad.

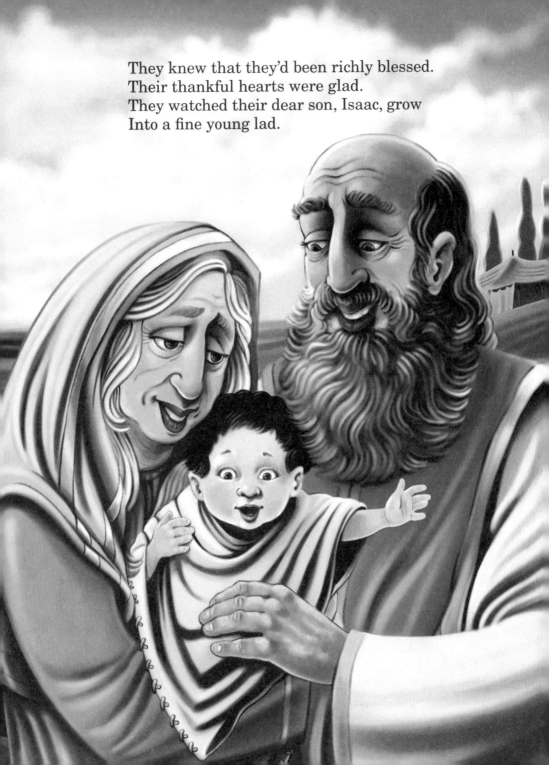

It was not long before God spoke
To Abraham once more,
"Take Isaac to a special place
He's never been before.

I'll lead you to a mountain high.
You'll build an altar there
And offer him as sacrifice—
Your son, your much-loved heir."

So the next morning, Abraham
Said to his son, "Arise,
We'll worship God up on a mount.
Let's pack up our supplies."

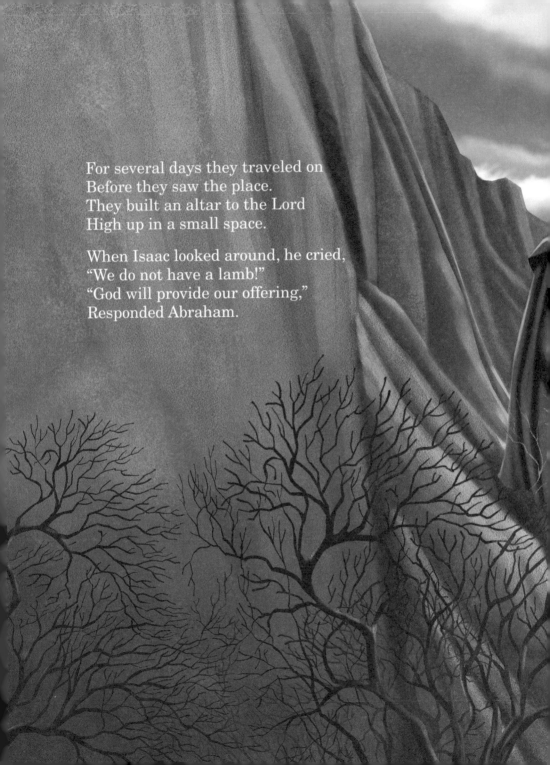

For several days they traveled on
Before they saw the place.
They built an altar to the Lord
High up in a small space.

When Isaac looked around, he cried,
"We do not have a lamb!"
"God will provide our offering,"
Responded Abraham.

Wood was stacked on the altar first.
Isaac was laid on top.
As Abraham took out his knife
A voice called out, "No, stop!

No need to sacrifice your son—
You proved your faith in Me.
See in the bush there is a ram,
So Isaac may go free."

They worshiped there, father and son,
And thanked the Lord above
For all the blessings they'd been giv'n,
For mercy, grace, and love.

Dear Parents,

What a marvelous story of faith and love, grace and mercy! When God asked Abraham to sacrifice his much-loved son, He was testing Abraham's faith. Because Abraham did not question or doubt God, he was willing to do as God asked. Abraham proved his love for the Lord and his great faith in God's plan for his family. He and his descendants were blessed, just as God had promised. However, the blessing was not earned by Abraham because he did good works. It was given out of God's grace, mercy, and faithfulness to His people.

It is important to point out that in Old Testament times, animals were sacrificed on the altar as part of worship because God instructed it. This was a way that God's people showed their love for Him and how they asked for atonement for their sins. Some sacrifices were used to provide for priests and their families, much like our offerings do today. But the main purpose of animal sacrifices was to remind God's people that a life had to be given so they could be forgiven for their sins.

Today we are no longer required to sacrifice animals on the altar as part of our worship. In the story of Abraham and Isaac, God provided a ram as a sacrifice. On Good Friday, God provided a Lamb as a sacrifice. This Lamb of God, Jesus, died on the cross to pay for all of our sins. We are forgiven because He died for the sins of the world. And we rejoice that He rose victorious on Easter Sunday.

To Him be the glory!

The author